Can You Believe?

INSECTS

by Sandra Markle

Illustrations by Jo-Ellen C. Bosson

SCHOLASTIC INC.

New York Toronto London Auckland Sydney
Mexico City New Delhi Hong Kong Buenos Aires

For our good friend Harold Gober and his son Ranger.

CAN YOU BELIEVE...

NOTE TO PARENTS AND TEACHERS: This book helps children become aware that, as living things, insects have a natural life cycle through which they are born, grow, reproduce, and die. Children will also see that different kinds of insects have special features that let them survive within their natural environment. "Plants and animals have life cycles that include being born, developing into adults, reproducing, and eventually dying. The details of this life cycle are different for different organisms." (National Science Education Standards as identified by the National Academy of Sciences.)

Can you believe

this mosquito needs a blood meal?

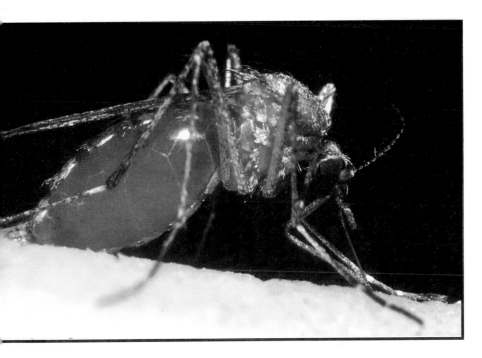

Just like male mosquitoes, female mosquitoes usually feed on plant juices. But eating a **blood** meal is part of the female's way of getting ready for the next important stage in her life. Like people, mosquitoes have a life cycle. They are born, grow up, produce offspring, and die. But a mosquito's life cycle is very different from a human's. That's because mosquitoes are insects—animals that usually have six legs and three main body parts: a head, a thorax or middle, and an abdomen. Insects also have two very special ways of developing into adults: They either completely change their body structure or they develop wings when they get bigger.

This book will let you investigate the life cycles of insects. You'll learn how insects get the food they need and how they survive long enough to have offspring of their own. Along the way, you'll discover some amazing facts about insects—some may even seem unbelievable!

So what will the female mosquito do once she's had her blood?

A. She'll die.
B. She'll lay eggs.
C. She'll grow bigger.

Turn the page and start exploring to find out!

Can you believe

the female mosquito lays her eggs after drinking blood?

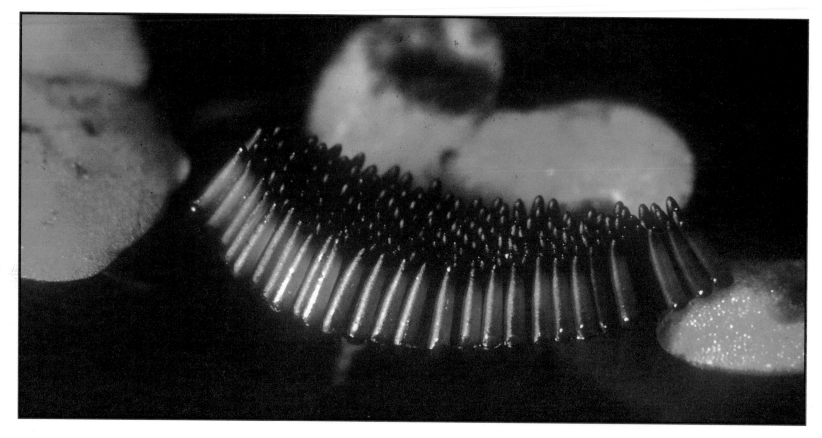

Blood is high in protein, something female mosquitoes need to produce **eggs**. Mosquitoes don't just bite people. They also get the blood they need from animals like horses and dogs.

Once the mosquito's eggs develop, the female lands on water and deposits them. She sticks the eggs together in rows, creating a floating egg raft of more than 200 eggs.

TRY IT YOURSELF!

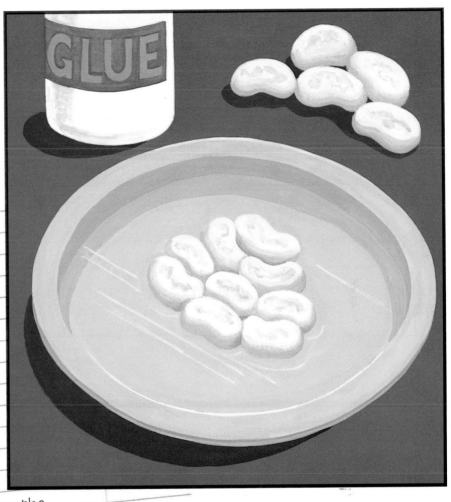

1. Fill a pie plate half full of water.

2. Create a raft of Styrofoam peanuts the way the mosquito creates her raft of eggs. Start with one row.

3. Next, add a row of two eggs behind it. Smear a little white glue on the sides of the peanuts to stick them together.

4. Add rows of three and four peanuts, forming a "V" shape.

The peanuts, like the mosquito's eggs, float on the water's surface. Water, like all matter, is made up of molecules, or building blocks, too tiny to see with your eyes. Water molecules naturally tend to cling together. At the surface of the water, this creates a sort of skin. Can you see why it helps the female mosquito that the surface of each egg is slightly sticky?

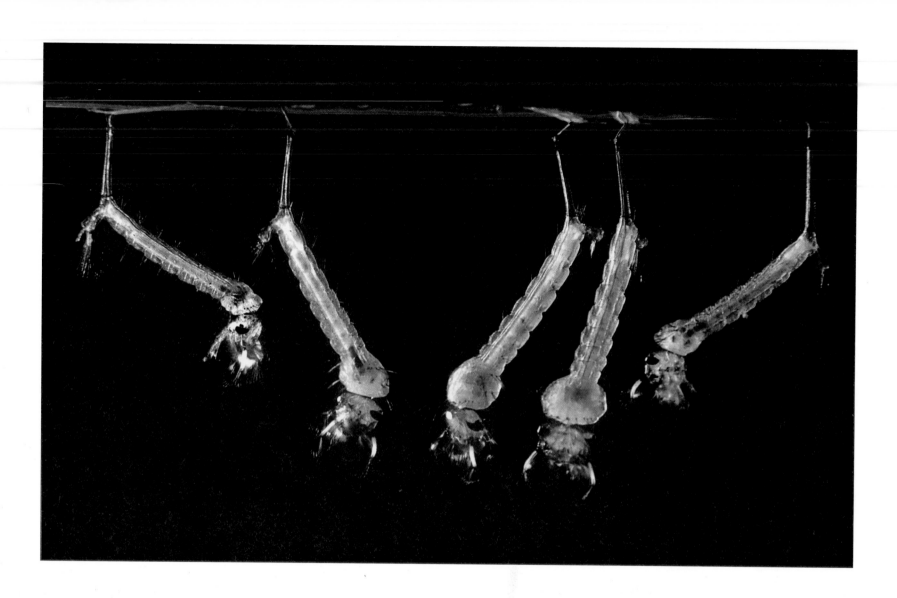

Why does the female mosquito lay her eggs on water? Because the eggs will hatch only when flooded with water. When the eggs hatch, young mosquitoes, called wigglers, eat algae and tiny animals that live in the water. However, wigglers breathe air. So they must keep coming to the surface. Then they dive down again to catch food.

Mosquitoes aren't the only ones that naturally know the best place for their young to grow up. All mother insects pick the best places for their offspring to be born. That's why this female moth is laying her eggs on a grass stem. When the babies hatch, the grass leaves will be the perfect baby food for her brood.

While most insect mothers just lay their eggs and leave, some protect their eggs from hungry birds, frogs, and other bugs. How do they do that?

A. build protective egg cases
B. put them in a safe spot
C. guard them

Can you believe

insect moms do all three?

Look at this female praying mantis building an egg case. First, she produces a special liquid that turns into foam when it touches the air. Next, she pushes her abdomen into this foam, creating holes. Then she lays her eggs in the holes. The foam hardens into a tough egg case. In areas where winters are cold, this also protects the eggs from bad weather.

See for yourself why a foam case is good protection against the cold.

TRY IT YOURSELF!

1. Pour a cup of water into each of two identical self-sealing plastic sandwich bags.

2. Press the air out of each bag as you seal it.

3. Seal one bag inside a second self-sealing sandwich bag.

4. Wrap the second bag of water in five layers of paper towels or ten layers of toilet paper. Seal this inside a self-sealing sandwich bag.

5. Place the bags side by side in the freezer compartment of your refrigerator.

6. Check your bag every hour until you see ice in the unwrapped bag. Take both bags out and squeeze the wrapped bag gently. It should still be soft, because ice hasn't formed yet.

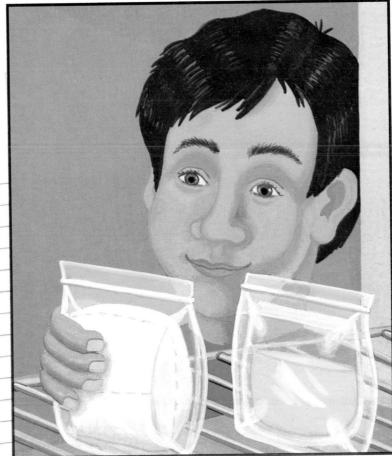

The paper, like the insect's foam, protected what was inside the bag from the cold. This is why foam is sometimes sprayed into spaces between building walls. It helps insulate the inside of the building from temperature changes outside.

This mother wasp is carrying dinner home to her babies. Her brood is safely hidden in a burrow. The female digs the burrow by hammering her abdomen up and down. Then she lays her eggs in the burrow. Once the young hatch, she keeps them supplied with food. She also cleans up after them, hauling away any leftovers.

A mother sawfly guards her eggs by standing over them. Her bright coloring is a warning to enemies to stay away. If a wasp or other **predator** comes close, she beats her wings hard, which makes a loud buzzing noise. If the enemy comes even closer, she lunges at it. As hard as she tries to protect her eggs, though, sometimes predators manage to grab some and eat them.

A female potter wasp does not guard her brood, but she builds a mud house to keep them safe. In fact, she builds each baby its own house—often as many as four in a row. Then she stings small caterpillars and stuffs as many as ten into each mud house. This will provide her offspring with the food they need to grow up.

Next, she produces a liquid from her abdomen and uses her legs to mold it into a cone-shaped cradle. She sticks this cone to the top of one little mud house and lays an egg in it. This done, she seals the house with more mud and repeats the process, laying an egg in each house.

A mother aphid gives her eggs a safe place to develop, too. She keeps her eggs inside her body until the babies hatch. That way, she can guard her babies and still keep eating. Once the babies hatch, the mother aphid releases them one at a time.

DID YOU KNOW?

Aphids are often cared for by ants. Aphids produce honeydew, a sweet liquid ants like to eat. In return, the ants carry aphids to leaves so they can suck plant juices. They also attack any other insects that come close to the aphids.

What's the first thing a young insect does after it hatches?

A. It starts to eat.
B. It travels to a new home.
C. It takes a nap.

Can you believe

young insects start to eat and then just keep on eating?

Butterfly or moth **larvae**, called **caterpillars**, may eat twenty-four hours a day. So it's no wonder this newly hatched luna moth caterpillar is looking for its first meal. Luckily, the caterpillar can eat the leaf right underneath it. Caterpillars have jaws with a hard edge. These act like scissors, snipping off bites. Once it finishes one leaf, the caterpillar will move right on to another leaf and keep on munching.

DID YOU KNOW?

Monarch butterflies have a built-in protection system because of the food they eat as caterpillars. Animals that have tasted a monarch once won't try it again. The butterfly's bad taste comes from the chemicals in the milkweed plants it eats as a caterpillar.

So what happens to a caterpillar after it does all that eating?

A. It bursts.
B. It sheds its skin.
C. It goes to sleep.

Can you believe

a caterpillar sheds its skin?

Here you can see this process, called **molting**, in action. A human's supporting framework is inside the body. But insects have an **exoskeleton**, a tough supporting coat on the outside of their bodies. Imagine growing bigger inside your clothes! When a caterpillar's exoskeleton gets tight, its body gives off special juices to separate it from the soft tissue underneath. Then the exoskeleton splits open and the caterpillar crawls out. Finally, the caterpillar swallows air or water to help it swell as big as possible. That will give it some extra growing room once its new exoskeleton hardens.

DID YOU KNOW?

Some caterpillars actually eat their molted skin.

Can you spot the caterpillar in this picture? It's **camouflaged**, which means it's just the right shape and color to blend into its surroundings.

Why do you think being camouflaged helps a young insect grow up?

A. It can hide from predators.
B. It can eat more.
C. It can become an adult faster.

Can you believe

being camouflaged helps the caterpillar hide in plain sight?

Did you spot the bagworm caterpillar's head? The rest of the caterpillar's body is inside its camouflaged bag. Shortly after it hatched, the caterpillar spun some **silk** to start building a bag around itself. Next, it used its jaws to press pine needles, bits of bark, and small twigs to this sticky silk. As the caterpillar grew bigger, it spun more silk and added this onto its camouflaged bag. By looking like just a bit of debris, the bagworm caterpillar is less likely to be spotted by a hungry bird.

This spicebush swallowtail caterpillar is camouflaged, too. But if a bird or other predator gets too close, it gets a big surprise. The caterpillar suddenly raises its head end, revealing eyespots that look like snake eyes. Hopefully, its enemy will be startled enough to leave the caterpillar alone.

These wasp caterpillars stay safe by hiding inside their food—the body of another caterpillar. The mother wasp injected her eggs into the caterpillar so the young would hatch surrounded by food. But being inside the bigger caterpillar gives the young wasps a safe home, too. The host caterpillar has protective coloring and stinging hairs to keep it from being attacked by hungry birds. Meanwhile, the young wasps dine on the caterpillar's soft body parts. Finally, the young wasps get too big to stay inside their host any longer.

DID YOU KNOW?

Scientists have discovered more than one million different kinds of insects.

You may be surprised to learn that these ants are helping this oak blue caterpillar. What are they doing for it?

A. They're bringing it food.
B. They're keeping away enemies.
C. They're building it a home.

Can you believe

the ants are keeping enemies away from the caterpillar?

The ants have powerful jaws and are quick to attack. As long as the ants are around, the caterpillar is safe from wasps that might inject their eggs into its body. So why do the ants hang around the caterpillar? The caterpillar gives off a sweet liquid the ants like to eat.

These are weaver ants, and what looks like a white worm is actually a larva. The adult ants do something special to keep their young safe. What do they do?

A. cover them with poison
B. stick them inside a caterpillar
C. build them a home

Can you believe

weaver ants build a leaf nest?

See the white threads stretching between the two sides of the leaf? These are sticky silk. Weaver ants build a nest by stitching two edges of a curled leaf together. An adult ant can't produce silk, but a larva can. So to stitch the leaf edges together, an adult holds a larva against the leaf and squeezes. The larva produces a drop of silk. Next, the adult moves the larva, tugging the silk glob into a sticky thread. Once the nest is done, the larva is moved inside. There it is cared for until it changes into an adult.

Paper wasps build a paper nest to protect their larvae. To make paper, the wasps use their jaws to scrape up wood fibers from fences or wooden buildings. Or they collect fibers by chewing paper products, like grocery bags and cardboard boxes. The wasp chews this fiber, mixing it with some water it drank earlier. Then it carries home the ball of wood paste. There, the wasp uses its jaws and legs to spread out the paste, forming a flake of paper. Bit by bit, the paper wasp builds a few cup-shaped cells where she can lay her eggs. This wasp queen starts the nest and catches the caterpillars or other insects needed to feed the first brood.

As soon as these offspring become adults, they take over construction. The queen stays home, laying eggs in the new paper cells that the workers build. As the paper nest grows, so does the wasp **colony**. In places where winters are cold, the wasps abandon their paper nests in the late fall and die. Only young queens survive and hibernate until spring. Then they start the process of nest- and colony-building all over again.

DID YOU KNOW?

Some wasps cover the outside of their nest with paper sheets. These layers and the air spaces in between become insulation. They keep the inside of the nest from getting too hot or too cold.

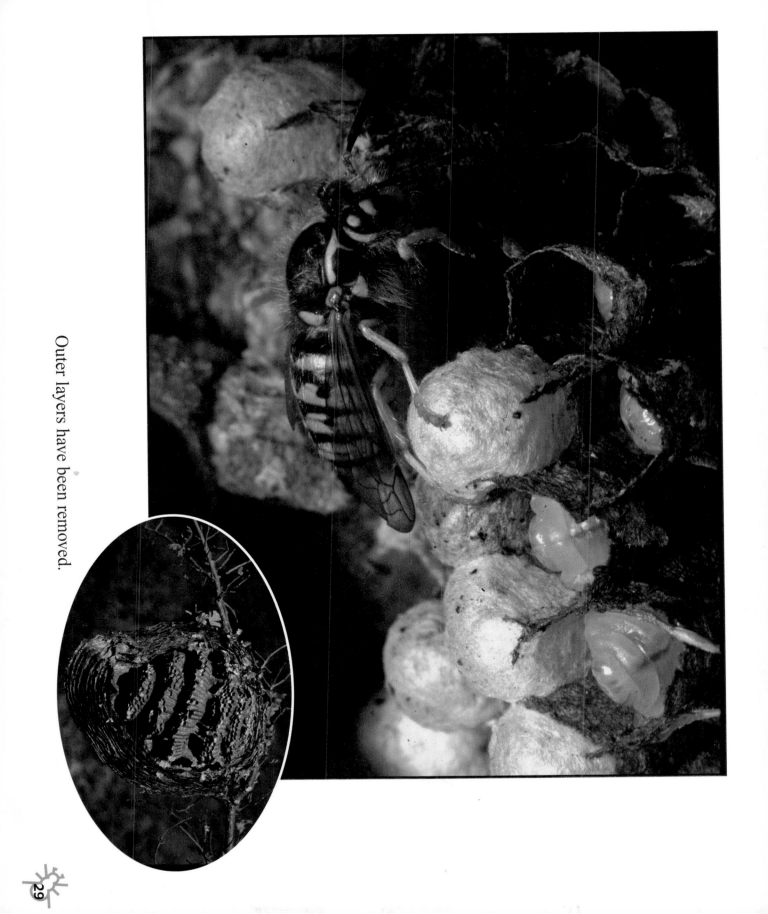

Outer layers have been removed.

TRY IT YOURSELF!

See what it's like to make paper.

1. Tear 20 sheets of newspaper into tiny pieces.

2. Soak in a bowl of water overnight. Cover your work area, wear old clothes, and work with an adult partner because the next step can be messy.

3. Have your partner cut a 6-inch (15-cm) square of window screen (available at hardware stores). Use scissors to cut waxed paper squares the same size.

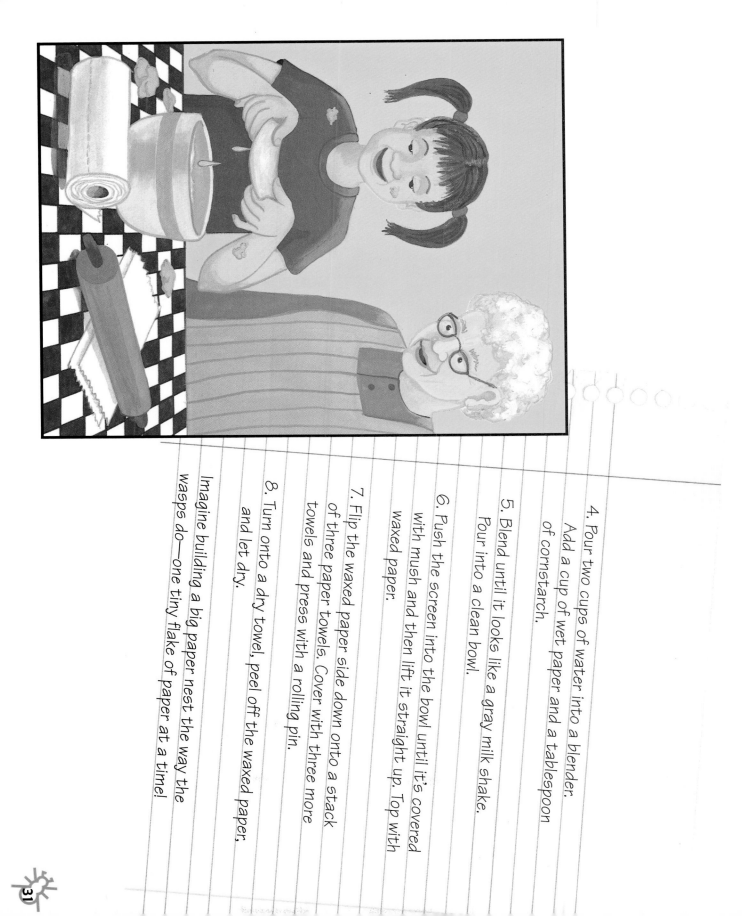

4. Pour two cups of water into a blender. Add a cup of wet paper and a tablespoon of cornstarch.

5. Blend until it looks like a gray milk shake. Pour into a clean bowl.

6. Push the screen into the bowl until it's covered with mush and then lift it straight up. Top with waxed paper.

7. Flip the waxed paper side down onto a stack of three paper towels. Cover with three more towels and press with a rolling pin.

8. Turn onto a dry towel, peel off the waxed paper, and let dry.

Imagine building a big paper nest the way the wasps do—one tiny flake of paper at a time!

Honeybees live in a colony, too. They produce flakes of wax from their abdomen. They use this wax to build a hive with six-sided cells that are just the right size for the larva to develop. Here you can peek inside a hive to see the wormlike honeybee larvae. See how each larva has a cell of its own?

These baby bees are just a day old. They are each in a pool of milky liquid food called **royal jelly**. The worker bees supply this food from special body parts in their heads. After about three days, most of the baby bees are switched from royal jelly to a mixture of honey and **pollen**, special grains produced by flowers. Those larvae will become new workers. However, when the colony needs a new queen, the workers randomly choose a larva to keep feeding royal jelly. That larva will become a queen bee capable of laying eggs.

So how does a bee larvae turn into an adult bee?

A. their body systems change
B. their bodies sprout wings
C. their bodies turn inside out

Can you believe

a bee larva's body systems change completely?

Just as people are babies, children, and then adults, an insect goes through several stages during its life cycle. Some insects look and behave completely differently during each stage: larva, **pupa**, and adult. These insects are said to have a **complete metamorphosis**. You've already seen what honeybees look like as larvae. After about five molts, the larvae are ready for the next stage. So the worker bees cap the cells with wax. Then each larva molts one more time, becoming a pupa. During this stage, the young bee doesn't eat and is largely inactive. All of its energy is being used to transform its body systems and its whole body structure into those of an adult.

Here, the wax caps on the cells have been removed so you can see the honeybee pupae becoming adults. Those with large, dark eyes are closest to completing the change.

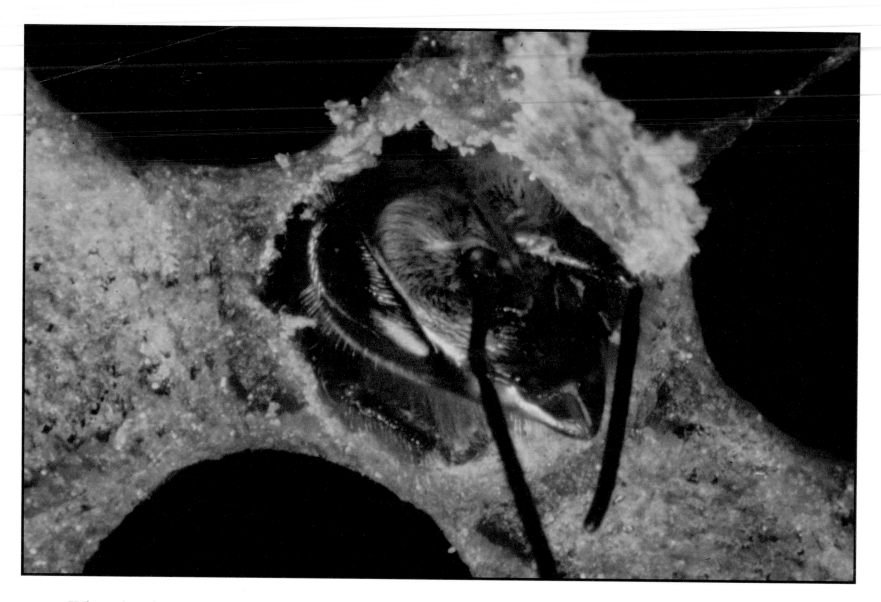

When the changes are complete, the adult bee chews through the wax cap and crawls out. Now, the honeybee is ready to start the adult stage of its life cycle. Look at all the ways the adult has changed since it was a larva and a pupa!

Remember the mosquito larvae that hatched in the water? After about four molts, they go into a pupa stage, too. Even though they're no longer wiggling and catching food, the pupae still need to breathe air. So the pupae float at the surface and breathe through two tubes. After about four days, the pupa's case splits open and the adult crawls out. Now the adult mosquito has wings so it can fly away. Instead of jaws, it also has mouthparts for piercing and sucking—just right for sucking plant juices and for a female to get a blood meal.

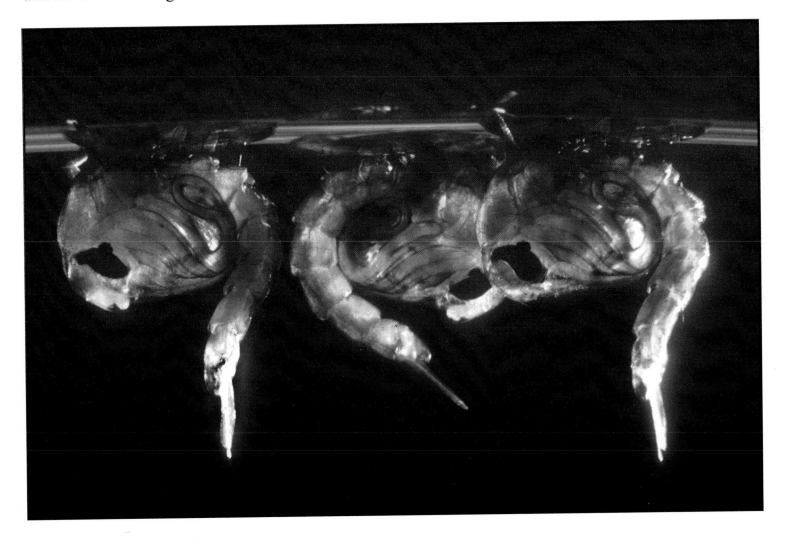

SEE IT YOURSELF!

You can watch butterflies or moths go through complete metamorphosis.

1. When it's summer, look for caterpillars on plants.

2. Put on gloves to protect your hands and gently move the caterpillar to a quart-size jar.

3. Add a sturdy twig for the caterpillar to climb on and lots of the leaves the caterpillar was eating.

4. Cover the jar with plastic wrap secured with a rubber band. Punch lots of small holes in the plastic with a sharp pencil to let in fresh air.

5. Add more leaves as needed until the caterpillar changes into a pupa.

How long does it take for the pupa to become an adult? Once that happens, take the butterfly or moth back to where you found the caterpillar and set it free.

Watch this butterfly go through a complete metamorphosis.

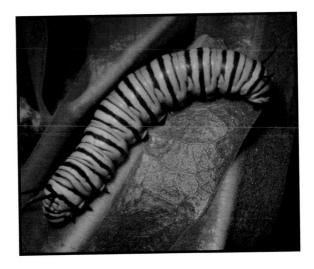

larva

pupa

adult

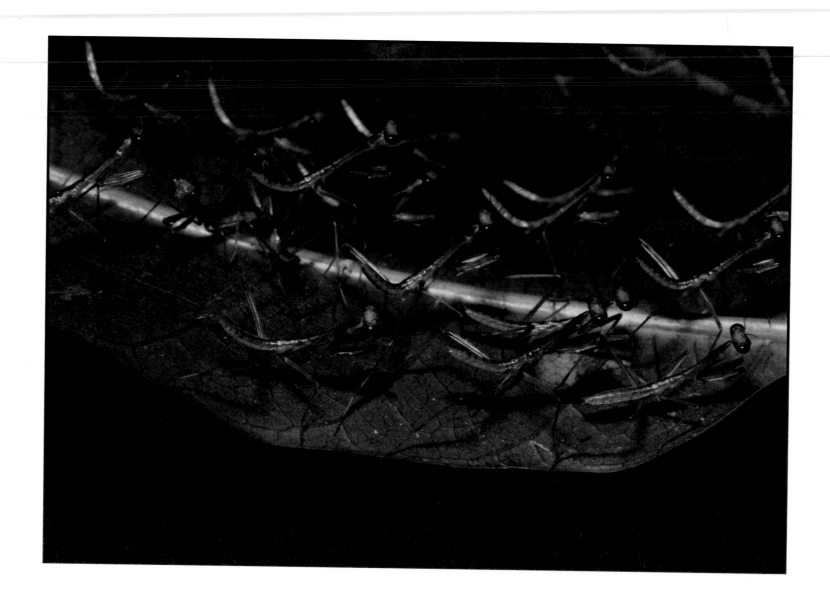

Some insects, like praying mantises, only change a little bit as they grow up. Look at these newly hatched young, called **nymphs**. They look just like the adults, complete with wing buds. The nymphs also behave just like adults. They usually even eat the same kind of food. So these insects are said to go through **incomplete metamorphosis**.

Remember the foamlike egg case that the female praying mantis produced? If you find one, you can put it in a quart jar covered with clear wrap punched with holes and watch the young praying mantis hatch. Place the jar where it will stay about the same temperature as the outdoors. That way, if you find the egg case in the fall, the young won't hatch until spring (the eggs hatch when the temperature gets warmer) when there are other insects for them to catch and eat.

DID YOU KNOW?

Once insects hatch they usually mature within days or weeks. However, cicada nymphs can take as long as 17 years to become adults.

In this picture, Laura Harrington is collecting mosquito larvae. She's part of a team of insect detectives trying to stop the spread of dengue, one of the world's top ten killer diseases. So far, there's no cure and no vaccine for this disease. The only way to stop its spread is to control *Aedes aegypti* mosquitoes. These mosquitoes bite someone who is sick and then spread the disease by biting someone else. Because spraying to kill mosquitoes is costly and takes a lot of effort, communities need to know how big an area to spray. So researchers are trying to figure out how far the mosquitoes travel between blood meals.

To find out, Laura Harrington and a group of researchers went to Thailand, where dengue is a serious problem. First, they collected samples of human cheek skin cells. This let them make a DNA "fingerprint" for each villager. Next, the team collected adult female mosquitoes and analyzed the blood in their gut. Harrington said, "Once we matched the blood's DNA with our database, we knew whom the mosquito had bitten."

Besides advising communities about how big an area to spray to kill mosquitoes, the scientists taught people the importance of getting rid of water storage jars. These open jars were likely to become mosquito nurseries. Often one of the most important things scientists can do to stop insect pests is to help people understand the insects' life cycle.

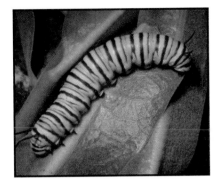

Can you believe

insects are part of Earth's cycle of life?

Some insects go through complete metamorphosis and others go through incomplete metamorphosis. But once they become adults, the next step is always the same—to **mate** and produce more young. So, an insect's life cycle begins again. Generation after generation, insects are part of the continuing cycle of life on Earth.

Glossary/Index/Pronunciation Guide

blood A liquid that transports food nutrients and oxygen throughout the body and carries wastes away. 3

camouflage [KAM-oh-flahj] Colors or patterns that make it possible to blend in with the surroundings. 19–21

caterpillar [KAT-er-pil-er] A name often given to the larva of either butterflies or moths. 17–25, 38–39

colony [KAHL-uh-nee] A group of insects or other animals living and working together for the common good. 28–29, 32–36

complete metamorphosis [kum-PLEET meh-tuh-MOR-fuh-sis] The process in which developing insect young have their body structure and systems completely change as they become adults. They pass through three different life stages: larva, pupa, and adult. 35–39

egg Female reproductive cell. 4–15, 25

exoskeleton [ek-soh-SKEHL-uh-tuhn] The tough, external supporting structure of an insect. 18

incomplete metamorphosis The process in which insects become adults by growing bigger, developing wings, and becoming able to reproduce. They only go through two stages: nymph and adult. 40–41

larva [LAHR-vuh] The name given to insect young that go through a pupal stage as they become adults. 17–25, 33, 39

mate A partner for producing offspring, or the process of male and female insects and other animals coming together to produce offspring. 45

molt To shed an old exoskeleton. 18, 35

nymph [NIMF] The name given to insect young that don't pass through a pupal stage and often look like tiny adults. 40–41

pollen [PAHL-luhn] Special grains produced by flowering plants as part of their reproductive process; insects and other animals sometimes use this as food. 33

predator [PREH-duh-tuhr] An animal that hunts other animals for food. 19–23

pupa [PYOO-puh] The nonfeeding stage between larva and adult when the body structure and systems change into those of an adult. 34–39

royal jelly A food that is produced in the heads of honeybee workers and then fed to the larvae. All larvae are given this for three days; those that are fed royal jelly throughout their development become queen bees. 33

silk A liquid produced in special body parts and then extruded. When it is pulled, it changes into a solid strand. 20, 27

PHOTO CREDITS:

Cover: Michael and Patricia Fogden

p. 2: Dwight Kuhn

p. 4: Dwight Kuhn

p. 6: Dwight Kuhn

p. 7: Ken Preston-Mafham/Premaphotos Wildlife

p. 8: Ken Preston-Mafham/Premaphotos Wildlife

p. 10: Ken Preston-Mafham/Premaphotos Wildlife

p. 11: Ken Preston-Mafham/Premaphotos Wildlife

p. 12: Ken Preston-Mafham/Premaphotos Wildlife

p. 14: Dwight Kuhn

p. 16: Dwight Kuhn

p. 17: Simon Pollard

p. 18: Edward Ross

p. 19: Edward Ross

p. 20: Edward Ross

p. 21: Brian Kenney

p. 22: Ken Preston-Mafham/Premaphotos Wildlife

p. 24: Ken Preston-Mafham/Premaphotos Wildlife

p. 26: Ken Preston-Mafham/Premaphotos Wildlife

p. 29 (2): Edward Ross

p. 32: Kenneth Lorenzen

p. 34: Kenneth Lorenzen

p. 36: Kenneth Lorenzen

p. 37: Dwight Kuhn

p. 39: Edward Ross (caterpillar); Skip Jeffery (pupa, adult)

p. 40: Ken Preston-Mafham/Premaphotos Wildlife

p. 42: Laura Harrington

p. 43 (2): Laura Harrington

p. 44: Edward Ross

p. 45: Edward Ross (caterpillar); Skip Jeffery (pupa, adult)

Acknowledgements: The author would like to thank the following for sharing their enthusiasm and expertise: Dr. Laura Harrington, Department of Entomology, Cornell University, Ithaca, New York; Dr. Raphael Didham, Department of Zoology, the University of Canterbury, Christchurch, New Zealand. As always, a special thank-you to Skip Jeffery for his input, efforts, and his support.

ISBN 0-439-35612-1

12 11 10 9 8 7 6 5 4 3 2 1   2 3 4 5 6 7/0

Printed in the U.S.A.
First Scholastic printing, April 2002